THIS BOOK BELONGS TO

TOYLAND

TOYLAND

CLASSIC ILLUSTRATIONS OF CHILDREN AND THEIR TOYS

BY
Pamela Prince

DESIGNED BY
Barry Zaid

HARMONY BOOKS/NEW YORK

Published by Harmony Books, a division of Crown Publishers, Inc.,
201 East 50th Street, New York, New York 10022.
Member of the Crown Publishing Group.

HARMONY and colophon are trademarks of Crown Publishers, Inc.
Manufactured in Japan

Library of Congress Cataloging-in-Publication Data

Prince, Pamela.
   Toyland: classic illustrations of children and their toys/by
Pamela Prince.—1st ed.
       p.   cm.
   Summary: Combines prose and poetry with old illustrations to
depict children and their toys.
   1. Toys—Literary collections. [1. Toys—Literary collections.]
I. Title.
PZ7.P9364To   1990   90-30488
                                                          CIP

ISBN 0-517-57619-8

10   9   8   7   6   5   4   3   2   1

First Edition

ACKNOWLEDGMENTS

I would like to thank my editors, Harriet Bell and Kathy
Belden, for their wise counsel and patient help, and for
generously guiding this book along its way. For their love
of children's books and the dreams they enclose, I should
like to express my appreciation to Ursula Davidson, Gloria
Timmel, Carol Docheff, and Garcia-Garst Booksellers.
Barbara and Terence Flynn, and my husband, Colin
McGlibery, deserve a thousand thanks and my love, which
I gratefully offer.

Toyland! Toyland!
Dear little girl and boyland;
While you dwell within it
You are ever happy then.

Childhood's joyland,
Mystical, merry Toyland!
Once you pass its borders
You can ne'er return again.

GLEN MACDONOUGH, 1903

INTRODUCTION

Our toys were almost idols. There was a glamour upon them such as we do not find in the more special possessions of our later years, as though a special light fell on them as through some window of our hearts that is now blocked up for ever. We loved them, it seems likely, not for any intrinsic beauty or charm of their own, for often they had none, but rather for a supernal loveliness of which they vaguely reminded our fresh and newcome eyes. But however that may be, we loved them with a devotion such as we shall never feel again for any of the things this various world contains, be they ever so splendid or costly.

O. SHEPHARD
The Joys of Forgetting, 1929

When I was a child my father used to sing "Toyland," in a soft and scratchy voice, to my brothers and me at bedtime. Now I sing it to my own little boy. Everytime I sing the words or hum the tender Victor Herbert music I find myself in a nostalgic reverie, recalling the seemingly endless possibilities and secret wishes of childhood. My yearnings today are certainly different from those I had as a young girl, when happiness was attained merely by playing with my favorite ballerina doll and fluffing up her frothy pink tutu, but the melody of "Toyland" carries me back to the always-longed-for and half-forgotten place where joyous adventures abound and dreams come true.

Donning his favorite black pirate hat, my three-year-old son is instantly transported to the roguish high seas where he clashes phantom swords and endlessly climbs imaginary rigging to an elusive crow's nest. His dapper wooden nutcracker accompanies him to the grocery store, to the park, and to bed; so, the most ordinary days and nights become enchanted ones. Children's wonderful beliefs and devotion to their playthings become the keys to unlocking the gates of Toyland, where gleaming towers and candy-paved streets appear, where talking dolls and dancing Teddy Bears magically come to life.

The artists whose images are included in this book must have nurtured a similar heartfelt belief in Toyland. I am grateful for their conviction that this lovely realm must indeed exist...and it seems important to pass along, to new generations, the beautiful pictures they created. Unless otherwise indicated, I have added my own text to enhance their visions.

I hope this collection of classic illustrations of children playing with their toys will intrigue and delight anyone who has ever traveled to "the dear little girl and boyland." Children growing up now will recognize themselves, even if their current toys are more complicated or sophisticated than the ones depicted here. The place itself remains gently and innocently eternal; Toyland is built anew by every child who hopes, who believes, who dreams.

As Molly placed Bunny Brady in line with her other toys she gave him a playful squeeze and shouted out, "The circus is in town! Right this way to the Big Top, my friends! What a jolly circus parade we shall make!"

12

GRIMBALL
Circus Parade

When Benjamin gently tugged on the string, the little wooden train began to move slowly across the soft, white bed.

"Look, Conner," explained Ben to his baby brother, "the engine and cars are leaving the station. Choo, choo, puff, puff. Over the snowy fields we go!"

HONOR C. APPLETON
The Two Brothers, c. 1914

13

Lillian Baker Sturges

T he shopman forgot to close the door!" exclaimed Jumping Jack to his friends on the shelves.

"Just once I'd love to gaze upon the real moon," mused the Fair-Haired Waxen Doll, while all the toys stirred and came alive. The Horse began to rock, the Duck waddled, and the Balls bounced when Roly-Poly said out loud, "Come, let's run away!"

A long the cobblestone streets they marched, under the light of the moon; and the sound of so many clattering, wooden feet soon reached the ears of all the sleeping children in the town. Bounding out of bed and opening their windows, the boys and girls rubbed their eyes in wonder at the colorful stream of bright and gleaming toys passing in the village square below.

LILLIAN BAKER STURGES
The Runaway Toys, 1920

15

Twilight Town was in the playroom, but the children had never seen it. They had never even heard of it, because it was a secret. But the fairy with the golden wand knew it was there, and she always came at Twilight to open the gate and set the toys free to talk and play together for one happy little hour.

16

One evening they decided to put on a parade. Teddy was the clown! He held a rattle in one hand and a feather duster in the other. Just to look at him made everyone laugh as he made funny faces and danced around. "March, march, march, march!" he commanded.

HENRIETTA S. ADAMS
MARY FRANCES BLAISDELL, Author
Twilight Town, 1920

17

Underneath the tree at Christmas time, a small, secret world took life so that if I bent down near enough I might hear Harlequin fiddle and the Shepherdess sigh. Candleglow mimicked starlight and my dreams were like the hovering nightclouds, pierced by a silver moon....

H. LEFLER and J. URBAN
Kling-Klang-Gloria, 1907

My wooden horse is brave and strong.
He can gallop and rock the whole day long.
In a red feathered hat and golden braid
I'll lead a line of soldiers in parade;
And we'll catch all the rascals, scamps, and knaves,
And anyone else who misbehaves.

19

FLOWER CLOTHES

I take my little china doll
And to the garden go,
I fit her there to hats and gowns,
But do not need to sew.

Our garden tailor has them all,
Just fitting, ready made—
The dresses are such pretty ones
I wish they would not fade.

The fallen hollyhocks make gowns
Of colors soft or gay,
And dolls may have so many kinds
All through a summer day.

A blade of grass will make a sash
And pretty necktie, too.
But best of all—on flower clothes
I've not a stitch to do!

CARMEN L. BROWNE
LOUISE MARSHALL, Author
Over the Rainbow Bridge, 1920

20

Raining, still raining! Oh, dear, oh dear! But what, you say to yourself, is a little rain? Jane Ann must be patient. She must stay at home and play with her delightful toys this afternoon, and then perhaps tomorrow morning the sun will come out, and she will be able to run about in the fields again. After all, it isn't every little girl who has a rabbit, and a horse and cart, and an india-rubber ball to play with. Come, come, Jane Ann!"

SAIDA (H. WILLEBEEK LE MAIR)
A.A. MILNE, Author
A Gallery of Children, 1925

21

Hope
Dunlap

Lucia blinked again and stared at the marvelous menagerie before her. "Could it be true?" she wondered. "It must be a dream. Every little animal and doll that I ever desired to have is right here. And a Jack-in-the-Box, too."

HOPE DUNLAP
The Rhyming Ring, 1919

Zachary put down the drum and patted Nick, his rolling blue elephant, on the head. There were real things happening out by the street in front of his house, and he took the small, red chair next to Uncle Maxwell's. "You know," said Uncle Max, puffing on his pipe. "Toyland is a wonderful place to visit, but this world here is quite interesting, too." So the man and boy peacefully sat, watching their neighbors pass by and butterflies fluttering over the blooming morning glories on the front porch.

ANONYMOUS
The Real Picture Book, 1929

Peter finally fell asleep
at a quarter to ten,
Dreaming of toys
and gingerbread men.

TORRE BEVANS
Dreaming of His Gingerbread Men,
c. 1927

I do not mean to scare or bite
Or give the doll a fearful fright.
I merely wish to welcome her."
Said Ted in his
most friendly *grrrr.*

ANNE COOPER
People's Home Journal, 1924

Why, Cozytown is the delightfulest place imaginable, 'though it does stand on the very edge of things, surrounded by a high, gray wall— that the name of this wall is "Facts" need not bother us, nor that to most people it is impassable. Those who know walk straight up to the wall and, taking four steps to the left of an iron ring which they will find without much trouble, they knock sharply on a stone which says BELIEVE! Presto! Immediately a little gate appears and in they go to the town itself....

On the way to rescue the Princess, a flock of angry geese chased the plucky toys of Cozytown and pecked viciously at their heels....

JANET LAURA SCOTT
RUTH PLUMLY THOMPSON, Author
The Princess of Cozytown, 1922

27

A ll set? Let's take off!" commanded Captain David, peering through his telescope. Eva waved her handkerchief. "Good-bye! We're taking off in the air-ship. See you later!" and little Andrea, below, imagined the table and chairs and ironing board and blanket floating like a zeppelin up and away over their house and above the rooftops of the town....

MATHILDE RITTER
Around the World at Play, 1932

Cotton smoke billowed from the chimney of the clothesbasket engine and Jake the signalman gave the sign. Carolyn hopped into the first-class passenger car, Teddy and the toys held on tight, and Ivan cried in the caboose.

"All aboard!" whistled Matthew. "All aboard for the Toyland Express!"

29

Marika laughed and straightened Fredrick up so that he might sit next to her on the throne. "Once upon a time," she began, "there was a beautiful Princess of Spring-time who lived in the woods with all her animal friends. There was even a funny little dwarf with a tickly beard, a shirt the color of sunshine, and a bright red cap with polka dots...."

RIE CRAMER

When I was sick and lay a-bed,
I had two pillows at my head,
And all my toys beside me lay
To keep me happy all the day.

And sometimes for an hour or so
I watched my leaden soldiers go,
With different uniforms and drills,
Among the bed-clothes,
through the hills;

And sometimes sent my ships
in fleets
All up and down among the sheets;
Or brought my trees and houses out,
And planted cities all about.

I was the giant great and still
That sits upon the pillow-hill,
And sees before him,
dale and plain,
The pleasant Land of Counterpane.

SAIDA (HENRIETTE WILLEBEEK LE MAIR)
ROBERT LOUIS STEVENSON, Author
A Child's Garden of Verses

31

One afternoon Alexander mounted the hobbyhorse in his bedroom and rode and galloped and rode 'til he came to a town he'd never seen before. Alex noticed that the stores sold only candy and toys and there was no one around to ever make a child take a nap....

LOUISE HELENE CALDWELL
Outdoors and Us, 1922

A ttention one! Attention all!
Hats on straight and stand up tall.
Left, right, left, a-marching go
When you hear my bugle blow!

BESSIE PEASE GUTMANN, c. 1920

33

Thomas really liked to take care of things when they needed fixing. He threaded the needle and stitched the clothes up quickly where they had torn. "Just be patient a little bit longer," he advised Daphne the Doll, "and you'll be ready to play again with the others."

MARJORY HOOD
Nursery Rhymes and Proverbs

34

Then the performance began. John played the musical box; I mean he turned the handle. Then Teddy did his dance. He was quite graceful, and every now and then he bowed to the audience. There was *great* clapping when he stopped.

HONOR C. APPLETON
MRS. H.C. CRADOCK, Author
Josephine, John and the Puppy,
c. 1920

35

Who would like a donkey ride?"

"Me, me, me!" cried they all.

Then there was a great drying and dressing again in the tents. There was only one donkey on the sands. We made Big Teddy be the donkey boy.

HONOR C. APPLETON

36

nd poor Amy tumbled down right under the sea, and got her mouth and eyes and ears full of nasty salt water. The boys laughed at her—Quacky, of course, began it. He pointed at her and said: "Don't ladies look *charming* when they tumble into the sea?"

HONOR C. APPLETON
MRS. H.C. CRADOCK, Author
Josephine is Busy, c. 1920

37

FRITZ BAUMGARTEN
Frohliche Weinachten! c. 1925

We know a nice girl who has been wishing for a horse just like that one," the three Angels remarked to Father Christmas as he painted one more white dot onto the little wooden steed. He answered cheerfully, "I think I know who you mean, and I happen to know she wants a shiny, red saddle and bridle on him as well."

38

BRITA ELLSTRÖM
Barina Hallonhatta, c. 1912

The red balloon carried Christopher up above the town, higher than the weathervane on the tallest church steeple, over the fields and lake and up into the realm of sky and dreams where he felt like a happy, floating, carefree cloud.

39

Mr. Waterman opened the door of his antique and curio shop, calling out, "Good afternoon, Devon. What can I do for you today?"

"I've come to ask you about a trade. I think the wooden ship you have here is beautiful. I don't have any way to pay for it so I thought perhaps we could make an exchange. I don't want to part with these toys but..." and his voice grew just a little bit tearful.

"Hmmm, I have an idea. If you agree to help me out today with chores, I think we could manage to give you the ship and let you keep your old toys too."

"Thank you, sir. I think that is a wonderful idea!"

GILBERT WILKINSON
Surplus Disposal, 1920

What are you able to build
with your blocks?
Castles and palaces,
temples and docks....

JESSIE WILLCOX SMITH
ROBERT LOUIS STEVENSON, Author
Dream Blocks, 1908

The Japanese Doll settled in among the silken pillows, ready to enjoy the tea party.

"Would you like a cup, too?" Sonya asked Bruno as he ambled closer to the table.

"Yes, indeed, I would," rumbled the bear, as politely as he was able. "With sixteen lumps of sugar, please."

W. LOGSDAIL
A Tea Party

As she prepared to leave Toyland, Franny passed a snowy cave whose entrance was marked by a warm lantern's glow. "Stop a moment, little lady," called out a band of tiny, wrinkled fellows in red. "We want to send back apples and chocolate for all the children." And the gnomes proceeded to load their bags and boxes onto her toy-filled sled....

ROSA C. PETHERICK
The Old Gnomes' Cave

43

She held the candle up high so that she might see all their faces one more time before going to bed herself. Blowing them a kiss, she asked, "Is everyone snug? We had a lot of fun today, didn't we, my dears? You know I love you very much. Good night, now, and sleep tight."

44

DORA McLAREN

S leeping little girls and boys
Dream of dolls and bears and toys.
 While asleep, do dolls and toys
 Dream of little girls and boys?

Playmates

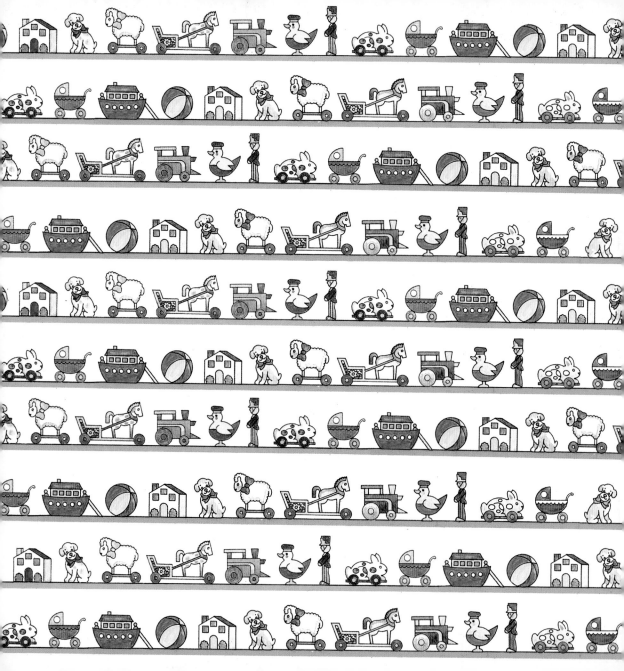